Jesus Is
Our Special
Friend

Wood Lake Books

The Bible is our special book
that tells us about Jesus.

Jesus lived a long time ago in a land with many hills and lots of sunshine.

Jesus healed those who were sick. He taught people about God's love, and how we are to love one another.

One day some mothers took their
children to see Jesus. They wanted him
to place his hand gently on the heads of
their children. This was a special way to
show God's love for children.

Soon they came to the place where Jesus was teaching. The children couldn't see Jesus because of all the big people in front of them.

Some of Jesus' disciples came and said
that Jesus was tired and too busy to
see children that day.

But Jesus saw what was happening and
he called out, "Bring the children to me.
God's love belongs to them. They are an
important part of God's people."

And he laid his hands on their heads
and blessed them.

Jesus loves children!
Jesus is our special friend.
Jesus loves me,
and you too.